MW00465447

THIS JOURNAL BELONGS TO:

___

Made in the USA
Monee, IL
04 April 2023

31326924R00115